Inside Eating Disorder Support Groups

Inside Eating Disorder Support Groups

Barbara Moe

The Rosen Publishing Group/New York

The Teen Health Library of Eating Disorder Prevention

Published in 1998 by The Rosen Publishing Group, Inc.
29 East 21st Street, New York, NY 10010

First Edition

Library of Congress Cataloging-in-Publication Data

Moe, Barbara A.
Inside eating disorder support groups / Barbara Moe
      p.   cm. — (The teen health library of eating disorder prevention)
Includes bibliographical references and index.
Summary: Discusses eating disorders in relation to support groups, the interactions occurring in such groups, what happens in a meeting, how to start a group, and the positive benefits available from such support.
ISBN 0-8239-2769-5
1. Eating disorders—Juvenile literature. 2. Self-help groups—Juvenile literature. [1. Eating disorders. 2. Self-help groups.]
  I. Title. II. Series.
RC552.E18M645 1998
616.85′26—dc21
                                      98-29942
                                        CIP
                                        AC

Manufactured in the United States of America

Contents

Introduction 6

1 Understanding Eating Disorders 10

2 Eating Disorder Support Groups 24

3 What Happens at a Support Group
   Meeting? 38

4 How to Start Your Own Group 44

5 Eating Disorder Survivors Look
   Back 54

Glossary 58

Where to Go for Help 60

For Further Reading 62

Index 63

Introduction

Amy reached into the mixing bowl, scooped up some raw cookie dough, and stuffed it into her mouth. That was good, she thought to herself. She swallowed another chunk of soft, squishy dough, then another.

Her little sister Meg skipped into the kitchen. "Okay, let's bake some more cookies." Meg stared at the tiny mound in the bottom of the bowl. She frowned. "What happened to my cookies? I need three dozen for my class."

"Shut up," Amy yelled. "You're such a crybaby. Make your own cookies." Amy raced to the bathroom, slammed the door, and put her fingers down her throat to make herself throw up. When she was done, Amy thought, What's wrong with me? I swore I wouldn't do this anymore. I feel like I'm going crazy.

Amy stared at her reflection in the mirror. Her face looked puffy and red. About six months earlier, she went on a rigid diet and lost a lot of weight. Her mom had taken her to the doctor, who expressed some concern over Amy's weight loss. After that, she'd started eating—a lot. But she felt guilty about it and began making herself throw up.

Dr. Murray had mentioned a support group Amy could attend. At the time she didn't want to. Amy didn't think she needed help. But now it seemed to Amy that things were getting worse, not better. Tears rolled down her cheeks and dripped into the sink. She felt alone and scared.

The doctor had pressed a piece of paper into her hand that day. "Here's a help line number," he said. "You can call any time of the day or night and someone will get back to you. It's completely confidential."

Amy turned away from the mirror. For the first time in months she felt hopeful. She would call that number.

According to the National Association of Anorexia Nervosa and Associated Disorders (ANAD), as many as 8 million people in the United States suffer from eating disorders and 86 percent of those are children or teenagers. Eating disorders affect mostly young women. In fact 90 to 95 percent of those who suffer are female. But an increasing number of young men suffer from eating disorders as well.

There is no single cause for eating disorders and no single cure. Most people try to keep their difficulties secret. But getting the problem out in the open and talking about it is the first step. And support groups can be that first critical step. Three days after Amy called the number her doctor had given her, she attended her first support group meeting.

If there is an ongoing support group for people with eating disorders, such as Overeaters Anonymous (OA), in your area, you can join one. If none exists, you might want to start your own support group. Many people of all ages also use the Internet to find online support groups.

Support groups offer many advantages. If you join a support group, you are taking a giant step toward helping yourself. First, support groups can offer members a way to regain control. Taking back control will make you feel good about yourself. Feeling good is an important goal in the treatment of eating disorders. It is important because many young people feel bad about themselves and their bodies and feel out of control in their lives.

Second, members of support groups receive strength from others who are in similar circumstances. Other people who are wrestling with eating disorders are likely to understand where you're coming from. Each support group is different, but one thing is always the same: members help one another.

Finally, most groups stress confidentiality. Confidentiality means that what you say in the group stays inside the room. Usually members exchange only first names.

This book discusses the different kinds of eating disorders, what causes them, who gets them, how they are treated, and how they can be prevented. The spotlight then turns to support groups for people with eating disorders. What is an eating disorder support group, how can a person find one, and how does it help? Taking a look inside a typical support group, readers will learn who comes to support group meetings and what the participants discuss.

You will also learn how you can start your own support group. You will hear from people who have recovered from eating disorders and how support groups helped them. At the end of the book, you will find a list of helpful resources.

Understanding Eating Disorders

1

An eating disorder involves a person' eating habits, attitudes about weight, food, an body shape, and other psychologic factors. It is usuall a symptom of other issues in a person's life, such as problem with family, friends, or school. It often starts at a point when great change is occurring i some- one's life.

During this period of great change, an eating disorder may develop as the person seeks control over something, such as his or her body, in life.

Eating disorders include anorexia nervosa, bulimia nervosa, and compulsive eating (also known as binge eating disorder). Compulsive exercise, or exercise bulimia, is classified as an eating disorder related problem. All are on the rise and affecting people at younger ages than ever before. Each disorder has its own characteristics, but a person can suffer from one or any combination of the four at the same time. They all present very dangerous health risks to a person's body and mind.

It is important to understand why and how an eating disorder develops. The sooner an eating disorder is identified, the sooner it can be treated. And treatment is essential in recovery from an eating disorder. According to Anorexia Nervosa and Related Eating Disorders (ANRED), 20 percent of those who don't get treatment will die from an eating disorder.

Anorexia Nervosa

Anorexia nervosa, usually called anorexia, refers to "loss of appetite." But the opposite is true. Those with anorexia are hungry all the time. Their weight is at least 15 percent below normal for their height and age. They are starving themselves, sometimes to death. But those with anorexia fear putting on weight and often see themselves as heavier than they really are.

Anorexia causes many physical problems. People with anorexia are frequently cold, even in summer. Because the body has so little fat, it can't maintain a normal body temperature. As a result, fine hairs—called lanugo—grow all over the body as a way to hold in heat.

Anorexia can also cause an early onset of osteoporosis, or thin, weak bones. Girls with anorexia suffer from amenorrhea, which is when menstrual periods stop. Starvation weakens the heart muscle, which causes a slow or irregular heartbeat. And dehydration from a loss of fluids can cause an electrolyte imbalance. This is very serious and can lead to death.

Anorexia also creates emotional problems. Because people who suffer from anorexia tend to isolate themselves from family and friends, they may suffer from depression. Lack of food can harm the person's ability to think straight and concentrate. It can also cause a person to feel irritable, unhappy, and pessimistic most of the time.

Bulimia Nervosa

Bulimia nervosa, or bulimia, is characterized by binge and purge cycles. Bingeing is eating a large amount of food in a short amount of time. Purging

A person may develop an eating disorder as a way to gain control over something—in this case her body—in her otherwise chaotic life.

is when a person tries to rid the body of the food by vomiting, abusing drugs that cause vomiting, using diuretics to force frequent urination, or using laxatives to cause bowel movements. Some people exercise excessively to rid the body of the calories.

Bulimia causes many health problems as well. Dehydration from purging results in dry skin and hair, brittle nails, and bleeding gums. Purging gets rid of food before nutrients are absorbed. Without these nutrients, the body can suffer from malnutrition. The teeth develop cavities or ragged edges from the stomach acids brought up by frequent vomiting.

When a person suffers from an eating disorder, he has less energy for the things he used to enjoy doing. He also feels alone as he grapples with the effects of the eating disorder.

Vomiting also puts tremendous strain on the stomach and esophagus. When the lining of the esophagus breaks down, an ulcer develops.

In addition, repeated use of laxatives can cause constipation (or the inability to have bowel movements without laxatives). Abusing diuretics can cause dehydration. Using ipecac syrup is extremely dangerous and can cause heart failure and sudden death.

Bulimia can cause the same emotional problems as anorexia. Because people who suffer from bulimia keep their binge/purge cycles secret, they can feel isolated and alone, and also suffer from feelings of depression.

People may suffer from more than one eating disorder at a time. Or they may go from one eating disorder to another. Fifty percent of those who suffer from bulimia have struggled or continue to struggle with anorexia.

Compulsive Eating

Compulsive eaters (sometimes called compulsive overeaters) are people who overeat in response to psychological stress. In doing so, they eat even when they're not hungry. Sometimes, like those with bulimia, compulsive eaters go on food binges. Some compulsive eaters graze, eating many times during the day or night. But they do not purge food from their bodies.

Compulsive eaters are often overweight. This can lead to problems such as heart disease and diabetes. But being overweight alone does not always cause these health problems. It's usually a combination of unhealthy eating habits and an inactive lifestyle. Emotionally, compulsive eaters suffer because their lives are controlled by thoughts of what, when, and how much they will eat.

Confiding in someone about your problems can help you feel better and more in control of your life. Your friend can also help you realize that you do not have to deal with your problems alone.

Just as with the other eating disorders, there are many possible reasons for compulsive eating. Sometimes it develops as a result of going on and off several diets. Compulsive eating is not about food but about a need for love. Sometimes people are cured when they begin to recognize and express their own needs and feelings. A support group is one place people begin to understand these needs.

Who Develops Eating Disorders and Why?

Growing Up

Puberty is the time when girls become women and boys become men. During puberty, it is normal for females to gain weight. This is part of the natural process of becoming a healthy, adult woman.

Unfortunately, changes during puberty are happening at the same time girls are noticing images of very thin women in the media, advertisements for exercise equipment and diet shakes, and magazine articles about how to lose weight. Many young girls believe this natural, healthy weight gain during puberty is bad, and they begin to diet.

Boys may also believe that if they don't look like the lean, muscular images they see in the movies, on television, or in magazines, they aren't good enough. In response, they might diet, abuse drugs such as steroids, or begin to exercise excessively.

The media is a large influence on how we see ourselves. When the media only depicts thin and beautiful people, we are left with the impression that the ideal body is one that is thin and beautiful. If we don't have the ideal body, this can make us feel bad about ourselves.

The Media

Young men and women are surrounded by images that project a body shape that is considered the ideal shape, but it's not a reality. Very few men and women actually look like this unrealistic ideal. Trying to reach the ideal shape is dangerous and unhealthy for most people.

When we measure ourselves against these images, we may feel inadequate, no matter what we look like. Advertising relies on and targets this feeling of inadequacy to sell us products that supposedly improve our appearance.

What is considered the ideal body shape varies from culture to culture, and is different at different times. In the United States 100 years ago, a pale and round appearance was considered healthy and attractive because it meant that a person lived well and did not have to work outdoors. Being thin and tan was considered unattractive because this meant a person had limited resources. In the 1950s and 1960s, Marilyn Monroe was America's most popular sex symbol. If Marilyn were modeling today, she'd wear a size 16—much larger than what current models wear.

We all have our own natural body type. Just as people differ in height and hair color, they differ in body shape and size. But because everywhere we look we see an ideal for women that is very thin and an ideal for men that is slim and muscular, many men and women think they need to change their bodies drastically.

Family and Friends

Parents and friends may buy into "be thin" messages from television, movies, and magazines. Big companies such as diet product manufacturers, diet clubs, and fitness centers hope you will want to lose weight. It's good for their business.

Mary Beth has bulimia. She traces its beginnings to a seemingly innocent remark her friend Emily made when they saw this flyer.

Needed
20 People for a Miracle Diet
Be Slim, Catch Men
Look Great in Your Clothes
Your Friends Will Gasp

"Let's volunteer," said Emily. "We've both bulked up a lot lately."

So Mary Beth went on a diet and lost ten pounds. However, within a few weeks, she had gained the ten pounds back plus five more. As time went on, her quest to lose weight became more and more desperate. She began bingeing and purging three months later.

19

Some people feel inadequate when it comes to sports. But with practice, most people can overcome their feelings of fear and have a lot of fun. Sports are a great boost for your self-esteem too.

Research has shown that the practice of dieting often leads to rebound weight gain (sometimes called yo-yo dieting), as well as to eating disorders. Every time a person diets, the body reacts as if it's being attacked. It stores fat more efficiently in order to function properly. The body's metabolism slows down, adjusting to the lack of fuel. So when a person stops dieting, he or she will gain weight because the body is used to surviving on less. Dieting also sets up an unhealthy relationship with food and can affect a person's self-esteem.

Low Self-Esteem

Sometimes young people feel depressed. Maybe you're not as popular as you'd like to be. Maybe you're trying hard to fit in. Maybe you feel inadequate when you fail to do well in sports or at school. In response to these feelings, you may eat food to feel better. You may try to get rid of what you've eaten. Or you may decide to take control by not eating at all.

Eating disorders are often connected to feelings of low self-esteem, especially when you blame and punish your body for the bad things happening in your life. Building your self-esteem is one of the most important steps in fighting an eating disorder.

Treatment of Eating Disorders

Just as every person is different, every eating disorder is different. Therefore, doctors treat eating disorders in

In order for treatment to work well, you will need to feel good about it. Your opinion really counts. Express your goals before and during treatment.

a number of ways and with a combination of treatments. Treatment may include individual therapy, family therapy, group therapy, medications such as antidepressants, education about the body and its functions, and nutritional counseling. People recovering from eating disorders must find the treatment that works best for them. It's important to stay involved in the decision-making process and be proactive in choosing the right treatment.

How Can We Prevent Eating Disorders?

Eating disorder prevention starts with you. It's important to understand that with healthy eating habits and an active lifestyle, your body will find the unique weight that is right for you. And this weight is determined mostly by your genes. This means your body size and shape are decided by the size and shape of your parents' bodies. You inherit these traits, just as you inherit the color of your hair and eyes.

Accept yourself as you are and value yourself for qualities that matter, such as intelligence, a sense of humor, and generosity, to name a few. Try not to define yourself by how much you weigh or what you look like.

Also understand that many leading experts now believe that weight is not the only factor in how healthy you are. What matters most is eating healthy foods and getting regular exercise—not a number on a scale.

Do whatever you can to express your emotions. Many experts believe that when people acknowledge and talk about their feelings and about difficulties such as childhood abuse or neglect, they are less likely to develop eating disorders. For some people this means reading books or watching tapes on how to heal. It may mean forgiving your parents and accepting the fact that they did the best they could. For some it means talking to a therapist or counselor. For others it may involve joining a support group.

2

One of the first national eating disorder support groups was Overeaters Anonymous (OA). It was founded on January 19, 1960, in Los Angeles, California. The three women who started OA had tried many other programs to help with their eating problems. They patterned their new organization after Alcoholics Anonymous (AA). The women admitted they were powerless over food. They sought the help of a higher power and the help of one another in dealing with eating problems.

What Is a Support Group?

A support group is any gathering in which people get

help from others and give help back. They accomplish this goal by sharing thoughts and feelings about their problems. This sharing helps them understand that they are not alone.

People with an eating disorder get used to keeping their difficulties all to themselves. They may believe they are the only ones with such problems. In an eating disorder support group, members learn that many others share similar problems with food, with friends, with family, or with low self-esteem.

Allie, sixteen, recently joined a support group. Cheyenne, nineteen, has been a member of the group for six months. When Cheyenne talks, Allie leans forward to listen. She says to herself, "Maybe in a couple of months, I'll be as sure of myself as she is." When Cheyenne listens to Allie, she says to herself, "Wow, I used to binge like that and feel gross afterward. I've come a long way." For both young women, the group provides a healing experience.

Belonging to a support group doesn't mean you'll always think exactly like everyone else. Sometimes two people disagree. But if communication problems arise, the members confront each other respectfully and work things out. Participants may discover that their old ways of relating to others don't work. In group, members can learn new and better ways to

There usually comes a time when each person feels comfortable enough to speak up and share his or her feelings in a support group. The group gives the speaker its attention and then helps the speaker sort out his or her feelings.

communicate. For the first time, many people are able to express deep feelings and to reveal secrets they thought were too shameful to tell anyone.

Before she joined her group, Jessica, fifteen, felt like she was going crazy. She would raid the refrigerator late at night. During her binges, she ate and then vomited whole loaves of banana bread and half gallons of ice cream. Her midnight refrigerator raids made her family angry. In group, she discovered she wasn't the only person in the world who did such things. Missy's brother hadn't talked to her since she'd eaten half his birthday cake an hour before his party. In group, Jessica and Missy laughed together about these incidents. The group laughed with them. Then both girls cried.

Support groups are an important part of the treatment of eating disorders. But they aren't the only part. Eating disorder support groups should not be substitutes for professional counseling. Dr. Eric Sigel, pediatrician and adolescent medicine specialist at the Children's Hospital in Denver, Colorado, says, "We definitely do eating disorder groups in addition to medical intervention, individual therapy, family therapy, and nutritional counseling."

Dr. Sigel says an after-school, day-treatment program at the hospital meets five days a week. Included in the groups are young people with all types of eating disorders. Inpatients stay in the hospital. Outpatients live at home but go to the program every day for therapy.

Those enrolled in the Children's Hospital day-treatment program begin their afternoon with a snack and meal planning followed by two eating disorder groups. The evening ends with dinner. "The groups are very successful," says Dr. Sigel. "Kids encourage each other in [dealing with] their various struggles. There's a lot of learning going on."

Support Groups

Although there is some overlapping, support groups

generally fall into the following categories: therapy groups, Twelve Step groups, self-help/support groups, and online groups.

Therapy Groups

In therapy groups, a mental health professional who may have organized the group acts as the leader. This person (often a social worker, psychologist, or psychiatrist) schedules the location, lays down the ground rules, mediates disagreements, offers insights, and sometimes gives homework. Some group leaders use role-playing, in which members act out (in the safety of the group) situations they haven't handled well in real life.

An important goal of therapy groups is to help participants understand and accept themselves as they are. Understanding and acceptance are first steps for members to begin changing their dysfunctional eating patterns. Sometimes comments from other group members allow participants to see themselves as others see them. In the example below, Sophie helped Ashley with a reality check.

In group, Ashley said she had stopped her binge behavior months ago. Sophie said, "Okay, then, tell me exactly how much money you spent on food last week." Ashley didn't answer, but other group members noticed the sudden redness in her face. Later Ashley was able to

Support group members learn from one another's experiences. They also usually feel a sense of relief learning that they are not alone and that other people care about how they feel.

take a look at her remarks and realized she'd lied not only to the others but also to herself.

To some people, for example, saying thanks for a compliment is easy. For others it is impossible. A friend said to Sarah, "That's a nice bathing suit." Sarah said, "It would look a lot better if I wasn't so fat." Role-playing in group taught Sarah how to accept a compliment with a simple, "Thank you."

Therapy groups can also be educational groups. For example, the therapist may try to help participants understand what triggers negative eating patterns. Keeping a diary may help participants remember insights they can share with the group.

Samantha revealed that a day of trying to diet usually caused a nighttime binge.

Rachel discovered that conflict, such as a fight with her mother, triggered a binge.

Alexandra realized that another girl's comment about her big, muscular arms was one cause of her anorexia.

Mark told the group that he'd given up chocolate, then ended up a few months later hoarding candy bars for a midnight binge.

Therapy groups come in many shapes and sizes. Some groups involve family members. Some deal with sexual abuse. Some take place in hospitals. But all have the underlying goals of education and support.

Sometimes group members feel safe enough to give the therapist or leader permission to videotape the sessions. Watching the tape later gives helpful feedback to members. They can begin to see how they are perceived by others.

Twelve Step Groups

Some experts believe eating disorders are related to drug and alcohol addiction. There are some similarities to alcohol and drug abuse: loss of control, experiencing cravings or urgings, secretive behavior, short-term relief of tension, and inability to stop the behavior.

For those who view eating disorders as a compulsive behavior, similar to an addiction, a Twelve Step program such as Overeaters Anonymous may be useful. OA is patterned after Alcoholics Anonymous. Both are organized around twelve principles that members try to apply to their everyday lives. The first OA principle is: "We admitted we were powerless over food—that our lives had become unmanageable." According to OA, all compulsive eaters have something in common: they are driven by forces they don't understand to eat more—or less—than they need. All who believe a Twelve Step program can help them, including teens, are welcome at meetings.

How do you know if you're a good candidate for a Twelve Step program? Use this list to decide if it is right for you:

- ❏ You have reached a point of deep desperation
- ❏ You have enough self-honesty to admit the truth about your situation
- ❏ You want to quit the destructive behavior for good
- ❏ You know you need help to quit
- ❏ Your interest in recovery is sincere
- ❏ You want what you see and hear in other recovered people

❏ You are open-minded about the idea of a higher power

You may decide that this type of program isn't right for you. That's okay. It's best to explore all your options before you decide which recovery route is best for you.

Self-Help Support Groups

Self-help groups are sometimes called mutual-help groups because participants help one another. Several persons with a common problem such as an eating disorder start and run these groups. The groups do not have a professional leader. Instead members usually share leadership duties. Every person in the group is an equal member.

Support groups are similar, but they may have an appointed leader, usually someone with special training in eating disorders. The leader's job is to run the meetings and keep the group going. He or she is not a participant. The leader may decide on topics for the members to discuss or may take suggestions from members. A hospital, high school, or university may sponsor a group.

In the meetings of self-help and support groups, participants talk about their problems with food, family, and friends, and with anything or anyone else that bothers them.

Julie says, "I got so tired of sneaking, and hoarding, and lying, I thought I might explode. Lots of times I did, and my family suffered. Now I get out my frustrations in group."

Self-help or support groups may occasionally sponsor a speaker. In this case participants may have to pay a fee.

Online Support Groups

If you have access to a computer, you may be able to use it for support. If you don't own a computer, you may be able to use one at your local library. Commercial networks such as America Online (AOL), AT&T, and Prodigy provide message boards and online support group meetings, sometimes called forums. In addition, the Internet provides self-help support through mailing lists that allow members to send and receive messages. USENET provides access to newsgroups, where messages are read, replied to, and stored.

Online groups have many advantages. One main advantage is near total anonymity. If you are shy and are not ready to attend a face-to-face group, going online may be just the thing for you. You can read the comments of others and even offer your own, but you do not have to reveal your identity. And how a person looks or sounds won't distract you.

There are many online support groups. Some people prefer the complete anonymity and convenience that an online support group provides.

Another advantage is that you don't have to leave your house. This can be a great advantage if you live in a rural area, far from face-to-face groups.

Other advantages include comfort and flexibility. Online groups usually meet in the evening hours, when you are most likely to be home from school or a job. At other times during the day, you may be able to find additional help in the message sections.

Be sure to use good judgment in online relationships. Don't give out personal information such as your address or phone number. Don't agree to meet someone face-to-face without taking precautions, such as meeting in a public place and taking a friend along.

Special Notes for Support Group Participants

Most experts believe eating disorder support groups have much to contribute to the treatment of eating disorders. In *Handbook of Treatment for Eating Disorders*, authors David Garner, Ph.D., and Paul Garfinkel, M.D., observe that most studies found group treatment of eating disorders to be as effective as individual therapy. According to these experts, group members seemed to make the most progress when they worked hard at the process.

Those who did such activities as keeping a diary and observing their own food habits made the most progress in group. Some people recorded such information as triggers to binges or how they felt after a binge. You can decide how much work you are willing to do.

When considering support groups, be aware of the following concerns:

- A self-help or support group cannot solve everything. Consider your group as part of an overall treatment plan.
- Don't believe everything you see or hear. Check things out. Talk to other people. Consider the qualifications of anyone offering advice. Get more

information from several health professionals.

- ❏ Volunteer leaders sometimes get overwhelmed with the problems of others. They too need the strong support of group members. If possible, rotate leadership duties.
- ❏ Although you need to have faith in your group, try not to get overly dependent on it. Remember that the purpose of a group is to help you function better in the world outside the group.
- ❏ Beware of any group that encourages you to hold on to your eating disorder. Beware of competitive dieting or group bingeing and purging.

How Do I Find a Support Group?

One way to find a support group is to ask your doctor, school guidance counselor, or teacher for suggestions. If no one you know can help you, contact your local children's hospital. Ask to speak to someone in the adolescent clinic or the eating disorder clinic. If that doesn't work, call other hospitals in your area.

Another approach is to look in the Yellow Pages of the telephone book under "Eating Disorders." Or you may find a community calendar listing support groups in your local newspaper. Radio or public television may also announce support groups.

At the end of this book, you will find a listing of national organizations concerned with eating disorders. In addition to telling you about publications and national meetings, these organizations may be able to refer you to a support group in your area.

What Happens at a Support Group Meeting?

3

You may be nervous about attending a support group meeting for the first time. Being nervous is normal and natural. Everyone feels scare the first time, but try not t let your anxious feelings keep you from going. Going to a group for the first time is hard, but other group mem bers will understand your hesitation. They felt the same way once. You may not say anything that first time, but the others will be glad you're there. No one will force you to talk if you're not ready. You can sit back and listen. You'll hear about problems similar to yours. Keep in mind that you will probably feel much more relaxed when you come out of the meeting. Going to the group will be much easier the second time.

Attend the meeting a couple of times, but if one group doesn't feel right for you, try another group. A closed group has a membership limit. If the group has reached its limit, your name will be put on a waiting list. Open groups have no membership limit. They accept new members at any time.

Other Factors to Consider When Choosing a Group

Here are a few more things for you to think about when deciding on a group:

- ❐ Is it close to home? If not, can I find a safe way to get there and back?
- ❐ What time does it meet? Will this fit in with my other activities?
- ❐ Do I feel better when I come out than when I go in?

What Do Support Group Members Discuss at Meetings?

Discussion topics at support group meetings are as varied as the members themselves. A leader or members may suggest topics. Here are some possibilities:

- Family relationships
- Feelings (anxiety, sadness, happiness, anger, loneliness, guilt)
- Stress
- Coping strategies (what works for you; what doesn't work for you)

When no one else volunteered, Tom offered to facilitate a meeting of the eating disorder support group he was in. He knew the meetings were better when the group had a specific topic to discuss. He began the meeting by telling everyone about moving out of his parents' house. As he was talking he hit on the subject of loneliness. "That's a good topic to discuss," said Tom. "Loneliness."

An eating disorder can make you feel depressed and isolated from others. A support group provides a forum in which you can deal with overwhelming feelings.

The word and its relation to eating and other life issues provided a focus of discussion for the whole meeting.

Discussion topics help with the sharing of ideas and insights. If you prefer, you can formulate your topics as questions. Here are a few examples:

- ❑ Since I developed an eating disorder, how do my family members see me? How do I see myself?
- ❑ How does my eating disorder affect my life? What can I do about this?
- ❑ How can I help others with eating disorders? How can others help me?
- ❑ What is the best thing about my life right now? What is the worst? What can I do about it?

After considering some of the questions above, ask group members for their ideas about other topics. This is a great way to involve everyone in the meetings and make them feel more comfortable.

How Is the Meeting Set Up?

Those who attend a nationally sponsored group will find a meeting format already in place. Local groups operate on various formats, but most follow similar structures. Here is a typical meeting structure:

- Members come in and others greet them by first name, if possible. If it's a large group, name tags will help. Everyone sits in a circle or around a table.
- At the designated time, the leader starts the meeting by making announcements and asking others for any additional announcements.
- One of the participants volunteers to read the group's purpose as well as any particular rules.
- The leader may ask participants to introduce themselves, especially those who are there for the first time.
- The leader may then introduce a speaker.
- If there is no speaker, the leader may suggest a topic. Those who wish may speak about the subject as it applies to them and their problems with food.
- Before the leader ends the meeting on time, he or she makes sure everyone who wanted to speak has had a chance.
- The meeting usually ends with some sort of closing ritual after which members may exchange phone numbers if they choose.

Who Attends?

If your group meets at a hospital adolescent clinic, a high school, or a college, members may be pretty much the same age. But multi-age groups can work too. At your meeting, you may have a leader, two co-leaders, or even peer counselors (people your age who have overcome their eating problems or who are in recovery). Together, no matter what background, participants help one another cope with issues.

How to Start Your Own Group

4

You'd like to join a support group, and you've looked everywhere. You can't find an ongoing group in your area. How do you go about starting one? Maybe you know someone else with an eating disorder. If so, you have the beginnings of group.

Kate met Rosie when they both were working as counselors at a neighborhood playground. They were at the sinks in the rest room when Kate said, "I wanted to take the kids to the pool today, but I hate to put on my swimming suit."

"You can say that again," said Rosie. "I know the feeling."

The girls met again a few days later and discovered they went to the same high school. Eventually they became good friends.

One night after a movie, Kate spent the night at Rosie's house. Rosie got out some ice cream and said, "I used to feel so lonely on Saturday nights that I would go on these awful binges. I'm better now, but I still feel the urge sometimes."

"You too, huh?" said Kate.

Soon afterward, Kate saw a program on TV that showed an eating disorder support group in action. She tried to find such a group close to home but had no luck. So she decided to start her own support group.

Plan Ahead

Who to Invite?

Most experts advise teens to get together with others in their own age range, if possible. Kate and Rosie decided they could also include college-age people. The girls each promised to find one other

If you decide to start a support group, try to find an adult who can help answer any questions you might have along the way.

person who would be interested in helping start a group. With four or five potential members, you can get a group going. Kate found a friend of her older sister who was enthusiastic and had lots of ideas. Rosie couldn't find anyone, so she put a notice with her first name and phone number in the church bulletin. As a result, the church secretary allowed the girls to meet free of charge in the church library.

When you make your initial contacts, be sure to ask for help in starting and managing the support group. It takes a lot of energy to build and maintain a group, so it is important to be able to rely on certain members to help you.

You may wonder about a maximum number of members for your group. Even if you're not limited by the size of your meeting room, ten or twelve people may be enough. If you get bigger than that, you may have to split into two groups.

Don't be surprised if your group builds slowly. If you have a hard time forming a group, speak to your parents or school guidance counselor about ideas for safe methods of finding new members.

Where to Meet?

Meeting places may include libraries, hospitals, places of worship, schools, and community centers. You could also meet in a member's home. However, public places are usually better if the group is large and includes people you don't know well.

Should We Name Our Group?

Your group can get along without a name. But sometimes when group spirit develops, a name surfaces. If it doesn't, you can have a naming contest.

Names often come from the group's location or its purpose.

What Time?

Working around people's hectic schedules, you will find no perfect time to meet. However, evenings or weekends seem to work best for most people. Kate and Rosie tried Saturday mornings for a while and then switched to Sunday afternoons.

Once you find a time that works well for everyone, try to keep the same meeting time each week. People usually find it easier to fit something into their schedules if it occurs on a regular basis.

How Long?

Sometimes if no one has much to say, an hour seems long. But when many people talk or when a speaker comes, an hour may not seem long enough. Most groups meet for an hour or an hour and a half once a week.

Your group may not last forever. On the other hand, it could continue for a long time, even years. People may be more willing to commit if you start with a time-limited group. For example, you could say at the beginning that this group will continue for ten weeks. Kate and Rosie's group started out with a twelve-week time limit. At the end of the twelve weeks, the group decided to keep going.

Who's in Charge?

In groups without a formal leader, someone has to take the responsibility for starting the group and stopping it, calling time on a person who talks for too long, sticking to the meeting format, or being a contact person. Most groups, even leaderless groups, need a contact person who takes phone messages, returns calls, and greets new members.

Will You Have a Buddy System?

Many support groups offer a buddy system. This is when a group member is matched up with another member who is available to offer support outside of the meetings. A buddy can be invaluable in helping you deal with your feelings.

Things to Consider When Setting Up Your Group

Although you may want an informal group, you will need some structure. Here are a few questions to answer before you begin to meet:

- What is the purpose of your group? An eating disorder support group should not spend time discussing favorite TV shows. After defining your purpose in a sentence or two,

Every support group needs reliable people to manage it. You will want to ask for volunteers, usually other support group members, to help handle any work that needs to get done.

you can tape it to a wall for all to see during the meeting.

❏ Will you ask for volunteers to start and stop the group on time?

❏ Who can join? What are requirements for membership? Can members bring guests? Do you want to include family members on occasion?

- ❏ Will you have dues or ask for contributions for supplies? If you decide to collect money, you'll need to elect a treasurer.
- ❏ What will your meeting format be? Will speakers be expected to volunteer or will you pay them? (Kate and Rosie found a volunteer speaker once a month.)
- ❏ Will you have a phone list so members can call each other for support between meetings? Ask the members how they feel about giving out their phone numbers before you create a list. If a member doesn't want to give out his or her number to the group, respect his or her wishes.

Group Rules and Guidelines

For any kind of group to work, rules and guidelines need to be created. You might want to think of your meetings as a job, for which you need to plan ahead. Here are suggestions for rules and guidelines that members should follow:

- ❏ Try to arrive on time.

- Respect the anonymity and confidentiality of all participants.
- Never talk when someone else is talking. Listen carefully.
- Do not talk about a person who is not present and never talk behind someone's back.
- Respect a member's wish to remain silent.
- Reach out in friendship and support to others, especially to new members.
- Use "I" statements (e.g., "I felt sad when Sally said . . .") rather than "you" messages (e.g., "You always misinterpret what I say . . .").
- Try to be positive rather than negative.

To Eat or Not to Eat During a Meeting

There is no right or wrong answer to this one. Someone in the starter group may have strong feelings for or against snacks. If not, vote. Food can be fun or it can be a bother. Decide if you want to make your food time purely social or if you want to discuss healthy eating while you share refreshments.

Your First Meeting

You've done everything you need to do to form a

support group and it is time for your first meeting. You're nervous. That's normal. Everyone gets nervous when starting something new. Remember that no one expects the meeting or you to be perfect. Be confident and prepared and know that you have started something that will enrich the lives of many people.

For additional help in starting a support group, contact the American Self-Help Clearinghouse, Northwest Covenant Medical Center, 25 Pocono Road, Denville, NJ 07834-2995, (973) 625-7101, http://www.cmhc.com/selfhelp, or any of the other resources listed at the end of this book.

Eating Disorder Survivors Look Back

If you have an eating disorder, you may feel as if you will never recover, that you will not make it to the healthy side of life. But with the help of support groups and other therapies, young people do recover. In the following stories, three eating disorder survivors take a look back.

"My family's message has always been thin, thin, thin," says eighteen-year-old Alicia. "In high school, I was totally messed up. Starting in my sophomore year, I began to think of myself as fat. I went on a bunch of different diets and lost a ton of weight. My periods even stopped for a while.

"That wasn't the worst part. After about six months of looking like a stick, I got tired of starving and started to binge and purge. Even though I threw up, I gained weight.

"A year ago, I found a therapist at the health center. She got me into an eating disorder support group. What I remember from this group was one person. I will never forget her. She was incredibly thin—like a dried-up skeleton with yellowish skin hanging from her bones. She looked more than half-dead. I said to myself, Oh, God, am I going to end up like that?

"From then on, something changed in me. I decided to change myself. It wasn't easy. But I realized I had to shape up or I was going to die a lot sooner than I wanted to."

Alicia's support group helped her to see herself in a different light. As a result, she was able to take control and make some positive changes in her life.

"A friend told me about an Overeaters Anonymous group that met at a hospital," says seventeen-year-old Maria. "When I arrived, I asked the man at Information

Many people have found support groups to be helpful in learning how to control their eating disorders and develop healthy relationships again.

where OA might be. He said he didn't have OA on the schedule. Off the cafeteria, I found this little meeting room. I said, 'Is this OA?' Two people answered, 'Sure is,' and they pulled out a chair for me. Eventually more people came.

"During the meeting, I didn't want to say I was anorexic. But no one seemed to care if I just listened to everyone else. At the end of the meeting, everyone said, 'Keep coming back.' You know what? I really wanted to. And I did."

Maria kept going back to a well-organized group that promoted the philosophy of living one day at a time. The group members offered her the strength and hope she needed to keep going.

"I wouldn't say I'm totally over my eating disorder," says Reina, seventeen. *"But I'm getting there. I go to a support group that started a few months ago. The people there feel like my friends. I've never had many friends.*

"At my first meeting a guy talked about starting a new job. He said he wasn't scared. He knew it would turn out okay. Someone else said they remembered him from six months earlier. Back then he was scared about everything.

"A girl my age was scared because she had to go to her great-grandparents' anniversary party. All of the relatives would look at her to see if she'd gained weight. Also she was afraid she'd pig out.

"It was good to know other people feel scared like I do. These days, thanks to the group, I can see the light at the end of a very dark tunnel."

Reina not only felt the support of the new friends in her group but also got some insight into the emotions all people share. You can recover from an eating disorder. But you may not be able to do it alone. Don't let an eating disorder rule your life. Through the sharing of thoughts, feelings, and coping strategies, eating disorder support groups can help.

Glossary

anonymity The absence of identifying information.

antidepressants Medications doctors prescribe to relieve depression.

binge To eat a large amount of food without control in a short amount of time.

compulsion The feeling of being psychologically unable to resist performing or doing something, regardless of consequences.

confidentiality Keeping information private.

depression When a person feels sad and hopeless for a long period of time.

distorted Twisted out of proportion.

diuretic A drug that increases urine output.

dysfunctional Not working properly or in a healthy manner.

eating disorder An unhealthy and obsessive concern with weight, body size, food, and eating habits.

genes The chemical building blocks of heredity.

nutritional counseling Counseling sessions where a trained dietitian helps a client with healthy meal planning and food choices.

peer A person your age.

psychiatrist A medical doctor with special-
ized training in helping people with mental,
emotional, or behavioral disorders.

psychologist A person with a Master's
degree or Ph.D. in psychology, the science
of the mind and behavior, who helps people
with problems.

puberty A time of rapid physical and hor-
monal development in both males and
females during adolescence.

purge To get rid of unwanted calories by
vomiting, taking laxatives, using diuretics,
and overexercising.

self-esteem The thoughts and feelings you
have about yourself.

social worker A person trained in providing
counselling service to people who often
have low incomes.

support groups Any helping network, such
as self-help or mutual-help groups.

therapist A person, such as a social worker,
psychologist, or psychiatrist, who helps others with emotional healing.

therapy Treatment of physical and/or emotional problems.

Where to Go for Help

Anorexia Nervosa and Related Eating Disorders, Inc. (ANRED)
P.O. Box 5102
Eugene, OR 97405
(541) 344-1144
Web site: http://www.anred.com

Eating Disorders Awareness and Prevention, Inc. (EDAP)
603 Stewart Street, Suite 803
Seattle, WA 98101
(206) 382-3587
Web site: http://members.aol.com/edapinc

National Association of Anorexia Nervosa and Associated Disorders (ANAD)
P.O. Box 7
Highland Park, IL 60035
(847) 831-3438
Web site: http://members.aol.com/anad20/
    index.html

National Eating Disorders Organization (NEDO)
6655 South Yale Avenue
Tulsa, OK 74136-3329
(918) 481-4044
Web site: http://www.laureate.com

Overeaters Anonymous (OA)
P.O. Box 44020
Rio Rancho, NM 87174-4020
(505) 891-2664
Web site: http://www.overeatersanonymous.org

In Canada

Anorexia Nervosa and Associated Disorders (ANAD)
109-2040 West 12th Avenue
Vancouver, BC V6J 2G2
(604) 739-2070

Web Sites

American Self-Help Clearinghouse
http://www.cmhc.com/selfhelp

The HealthGate Web Site
http://www.healthgate.com

HealthWorld Online
http://www.healthworld.org

For Further Reading

Ferguson, Tom, MD. *Health Online: How to Find Health Information, Support Groups, and Self-Help Communities in Cyberspace.* Reading, MA: Addison-Wesley Publishing Co., 1996.

Kolodny, Nancy J. *When Food's a Foe: How You Can Confront and Conquer Your Eating Disorder.* New York: Little, Brown and Co., 1992.

Kubersky, Rachel. *Everything You Need to Know About Eating Disorders.* Rev. ed. New York: Rosen Publishing Group, 1996.

McCoy, Kathy, and Charles Wibbelsman, MD. *The New Teenage Body Book.* New York: Putnam Publishing Group, 1992.

Moe, Barbara. *Coping with Eating Disorders.* Rev. ed. New York: Rosen Publishing Group, 1995.

Roth, Geneen. *Why Weight? A Guide to Ending Compulsive Eating.* New York: Penguin Group, 1994.

Index

A

abuse, 23

amenorrhea, 12

anorexia nervosa, 11–12, 15
  consequences, 12

Anorexia Nervosa and Related
    Eating Disorders (ANRED),
    11

anxiety, 38, 40

B

bingeing and purging, 12–15, 19,
    26, 35, 36, 45, 55

body shape, 10, 18–19

bulimia, 11, 12–15, 19

C

compulsive eating, 11, 15–16, 31

confidentiality, 7, 8, 33, 52

control, 8, 11, 21, 30, 55

D

depression, 12, 15, 20–21

diary keeping, 29, 35

diets, 16, 17, 19–20

diuretics, 13–14

drug abuse, 30

E

eating disorders, 8–9, 15, 23, 31, 36
  causes, 16–21

consequences, 11–16, 41
defined, 10–11
preventing, 9, 22–23
recovery, 11, 22, 32, 43, 54, 57
sufferers, 7, 11, 54–57
treating, 9, 11, 21–22, 27, 35

exercise, 11, 17, 23

F

family, 10, 19, 33, 40, 41

fat, 20

feelings, 8, 16, 20, 26, 38, 40

friends, 10, 19, 32

G

genes, 22

H

hospitals, 36, 47, 55–56

I

ipecac, 14

L

laxatives, 13–14

M

media, 18–19

N

National Association of Anorexia
    Nervosa and Associated
    Disorders (ANAD), 7

nutritional counseling, 22, 27

O

Overeaters Anonymous (OA), 8, 24, 31, 55–56

P

psychiatrists, 28
psychologists, 28
puberty, 16–17

R

role-playing, 29

S

secrecy, 7, 15, 26, 30
self-esteem, 20–21, 25
Sigel, Dr. Eric, 27
social workers, 28
support groups, 7–8, 9, 23, 35, 38, 54–57
  choosing, 35–37, 39
  defined, 24–25

discussion topics, 39–41
finding, 36–37
leaders, 28–29, 32, 36, 40-41, 42, 49
meetings, 38–43, 51, 52–53
members, 8, 25–27, 29, 30, 32, 35, 38–43, 45–47, 50–52
online, 8, 33–34
self-help, 32–33
starting, 9, 44–53
therapy, 28–30
Twelve Step, 30–32

T

therapy
  family, 22, 28
  group, 22, 28
  individual, 22, 28, 35

V

vomiting, 13–14

W

weight, 6, 10, 12, 17, 20, 22, 55

About the Author

Barbara Moe has a Bachelor of Science degree in Nursing from the College of Nursing and Health, University of Cincinnati, and a Master of Science degree in Nursing from Ohio State University. She received a Master of Social Work degree, as well as a certificate in Marriage and Family Therapy, from the University of Denver.

Design and Layout: Christine Innamorato

Consulting Editor: Michele I. Drohan

Photo Credits

Photo on p. 10 © Victor Ramos/International Stock; p. 13 © Mimi Cotter/International Stock; p. 14 © Spencer Jones/FPG International; p. 16 © James Davis/International Stock; p. 17 © Corbis Bettman pp. 20, 26, 40 by Maike Schulz; p. 21 by John Bentham; p. 24 © Stephen Simpson/FPG International; pp. 29, 46 by Ira Fox; p. 34 © Patrick Ramsey/International Stock; p. 38 © Skjold Photographs; p. 44 © Telegraph Colour Library/FPG International; p. 50 © Scott Campbell/International Stock; p. 54 © James Davis/International Stock; p. 56 © Rob Gage/FPG International.